GUIDING LIGHT:

A Journey of Mentorship and Destiny

A NOBODY DOUGLAS MAYERS

GUIDING LIGHT:

A Nobody Douglas Mayers
Guiding Light

Published by Spines
ISBN: 979-8-89383-272-3

CONTENTS

Chapter One

GRADUATION DAY

The school gate swings open as the year's final bell chimes, signaling another academic Year's end. Donella steps out into the warm afternoon sun, her heart heavy with relief and uncertainty. As she exits the school grounds, the dusty roads of her small Nigerian town stretch out before her, winding their way through clusters of mud-brick houses with thatched roofs, offering respite from the relentless African sun.

Surrounding these humble abodes stand towering palm trees, their fronds swaying gently in the warm breeze that sweeps through the village. Children play in the narrow streets, their laughter echoing off the walls of nearby buildings, while women clad in brightly colored garments balance baskets of fruit on their heads as they make their way to the bustling market at the heart of the town.

Donella's school, a modest structure of weathered concrete and corrugated tin, stands as a beacon of hope and opportunity amidst the simplicity of village life. Its walls bear the marks of generations of students who have passed through its doors, their dreams and aspirations woven into the very fabric of the building.

As she makes her way home, Donella passes by the village square, where elders gather beneath the shade of a towering baobab tree to share stories and wisdom passed down through the ages. The air is thick with the scent of spices and the sound of drums, transporting her to a world steeped in tradition and history.

Despite the challenges and limitations of her surroundings, Donella can't help but feel a sense of pride and belonging as she walks through the familiar streets of her hometown. For her, this small corner of Nigeria holds a beauty and richness that cannot be found anywhere else in the world.

. . .

As she approaches her family's modest compound, nestled amidst the vibrant community, Donella's thoughts turn inward. She reflects on the journey that has brought her to this moment, the countless hours spent studying, the dreams she dared to dream, and the unwavering support of her family and mentors.

Donella: (Internally) "Graduation Day... it's finally here. The culmination of years of hard work and dedication. But what comes next? Where do I go from here?"

As she enters her family's compound courtyard, Donella is greeted by the comforting sight of her loved ones gathered beneath the shade of a sprawling mango tree.

Donella's Mother: (Smiling warmly) "Congratulations, my dear! We're so proud of you."

Donella's Father: (Proudly) "You've made us all proud, Donella. Your future is bright, and we're excited to see where it takes you."

. . .

Donella: (Gratefully) "Thank you, Mama, Papa. I couldn't have done it without your love and support."

As the family gathers for a celebratory meal, Donella's siblings share stories and laughter, their bond stronger than ever in this moment of triumph.

Donella's Younger Brother: (Excitedly) "Donella, did you hear about the auditions for the community theatre production? You should totally audition!"

Donella: (Contemplatively) "Auditions, huh? Maybe it's time I took another leap of faith."

As the evening wears on and the stars twinkle in the night sky, Donella finds herself lost in thought, the possibilities of the future stretching out like the vast African plains.

Donella: (Internally) "Perhaps there's more out there for me than I ever imagined. Maybe it's time to step out of my comfort zone and explore what the world has to offer."

. . .

With a renewed sense of purpose and determination, Donella looks ahead to the future, ready to embrace whatever adventures lie in store.

Days pass, and Donella immerses herself in the world of auditions and acting opportunities, her determination unwavering despite her challenges.

Donella's small bedroom, tucked away in the corner of her family's compound, becomes her sanctuary, a place where she can escape the hustle and bustle of daily life and focus on her craft. The walls are adorned with posters of her favorite actors and actresses, serving as constant reminders of the dreams she's chasing.

Donella: (Looking around her room, determination shining in her eyes) "This is where it all begins. Every audition, every practice session—it's all part of the journey."

As she delves deeper into the acting world, Donella grapples with doubts and insecurities, wondering if she has what it takes to succeed in such a competitive industry.

Donella: (Reflecting on her journey so far) "It's not easy, but nothing worth having, ever is. I'll keep pushing forward, no matter what."

Despite the occasional setback and rejection, Donella refuses to give up, channeling her passion into every audition she attends. Each rejection letter fuels her determination, propelling her forward on her journey toward her dreams.

Donella: (After a particularly challenging audition, she takes a deep breath and reminds herself) "This is what I love. I won't let one setback stop me."

Through it all, Donella's family stands by her side, offering words of encouragement and unwavering support.

Donella's Mother: (Soothingly) "Don't be disheartened, my dear. Your talent shines brighter than any audition room."

. . .

Donella's Father: (Proudly) "You have the heart of a lion, Donella. Keep pushing forward, and you'll achieve great things."

Meanwhile, Donella's mentor, whom she addresses respectfully as "Boss" or "Sir," continues encouraging her to broaden her horizons. He urges her to send her CV for jobs in Nigeria and internationally.

Boss: (Over WhatsApp call) "Donella, my dear, the world is your stage. Don't limit yourself to just local productions. Send out your CV to international companies. You have the talent and the drive. They'd be lucky to have you."

Donella: (Gratefully) "Thank you, Boss. I'll do it. I'll cast my net wider and see what opportunities await beyond these familiar shores."

As Donella juggles auditions and rehearsals with her local theatre group, she can't help but feel excitement and anticipation for what the future holds. With her Boss's encouragement and her family's unwavering support, she knows no dream is too big to chase.

Donella: (Gazing out at the starlit sky, a smile on her lips) "The world is vast and full of possibilities. I'll keep reaching for the stars, one audition at a time."

Narration

With her mentor's guidance and encouragement, Donella feels empowered to continue pursuing her dreams, one stitch at a time.

Chapter Two

A LEAP OF FAITH

As Donella continues pursuing her passion for acting, she finds herself fully immersed in local productions with the community theatre group. Their rehearsals become a second home to her, where she can shed her inhibitions and fully embrace her love for the stage.

The local theatre group, known as Local Men Productions, operates out of a small, makeshift theatre in the heart of the village. The building may be simple, but it's filled with energy and passion that are palpable from the moment Donella steps through the door. The sound of laughter and chatter fills the air as the cast and crew prepare for their latest production.

· · ·

Donella: (Taking in the bustling atmosphere of the theatre) "This feels like home."

As rehearsals progress, Donella finds herself forming close bonds with her fellow actors and crew members. They become her confidants, her cheerleaders, and her friends, offering support and encouragement every step of the way.

Donella: (Sharing a laugh with her co-stars) "I never imagined I'd find such a wonderful community here.

One evening, as the cast gathers for a final dress rehearsal before opening night, Donella cannot contain the nerves. Their expectations hang heavy on her shoulders as she waits in the wings, her heart pounding with anticipation.

Director: (Addressing the cast) "Alright, everyone. Let's make this one count. Remember why we're here: to bring joy and laughter to our audience. Now, let's show them what we're made of!"

. . .

As the curtain rises and the spotlight falls on Donella, she takes a deep breath and steps into the limelight. The familiar rush of adrenaline courses through her veins as she delivers her lines with confidence and poise, each word ringing out loud and clear.

Audience members lean forward in their seats, captivated by Donella's performance. Their laughter fills the theatre as she delivers her punchlines with impeccable timing, her presence commanding the stage with ease.

Donella: (Basking in the glow of the applause) "This is what I was meant to do."

After the final curtain falls and the applause dies down, Donella finds herself surrounded by her fellow cast members, their smiles and hugs filling her with a sense of pride and accomplishment.

Co-star: (Beaming) "You were amazing out there, Donella. I'm so glad we got to share this moment with you."

.   .   .

Director: (Approaching smiling) "Donella, you were a revelation tonight. Your talent truly knows no bounds."

As Donella basks in the afterglow of their successful performance, she can't help but feel a sense of gratitude for the journey that has brought her to this moment. With each step she takes, she's one step closer to realizing her dreams, and she's more determined than ever to seize every opportunity that comes her way.

Donella: (Looking out at the empty stage, a smile playing on her lips) "This is just the beginning. And I can't wait to see where the road ahead takes me."

Chapter Three

EMBRACING OPPORTUNITIES

As Donella dives into rehearsals for the regional theatre company's production, she surrounds herself with a diverse group of talented actors and actresses. Each rehearsal brings new challenges and opportunities for growth, and Donella throws herself into her work with determination and enthusiasm.

Rehearsal Room:

Director: (Addressing the cast) "Alright, everyone. Let's dive into Act 1, Scene 2. Donella, I'd like to work on your blocking for this scene today."

Donella: (Nodding eagerly) "Of course, Director. I'm ready."

· · ·

As the scene unfolds, Donella immerses herself in her character, bringing depth and emotion to her performance. She gracefully takes direction from the director, adjusting her movements and expressions to serve the scene better.

Co-star: (Offering feedback) "Donella, that was fantastic. I love the way you're approaching this character."

Donella: (Gratefully) "Thank you. I'm trying to really inhabit her and bring her to life."

During rehearsal breaks, Donella bonds with her fellow actors, sharing stories and laughter as they work together to bring the production to life.

Donella: (Laughing with her co-stars) I can't believe we're actually doing this. It's a dream come true.

Co-star: (Smiling) You're a natural, Donella. I'm so glad we get to share the stage together.

· · ·

As opening night draws nearer, Donella reflects on her journey and the road that has led her to this moment. She thinks back to the small theatre in her hometown, the auditions she attended, and the countless hours she spent honing her craft.

Donella: (Looking out at the empty stage, a sense of wonder in her eyes) "Who would have thought that a girl from a small town in Nigeria would end up here? It's surreal."

Despite her nerves, Donella feels excitement building within her. She knows this production is just the beginning of what promises to be an incredible journey, and she's ready to embrace every moment.

Donella: (Taking a deep breath and a smile playing on her lips) "Here's to new beginnings and the adventures that lie ahead. I'm ready for whatever comes my way."

Donella enters the spotlight with confidence and grace as the lights dim and the curtain rises on opening night. With each line she delivers and every emotion she portrays, she knows she's exactly where she's meant to be onstage, doing what she loves and living her dream.

Donella: (In character, delivering her lines with conviction) "This is it. This is my moment."

As the audience erupts into applause at the end of the performance, Donella, with a sense of fulfillment washed over her. She recognizes she's found her place in the theatre world and can't wait to see where this journey takes her next.

Chapter Four

A TIME FOR REFLECTION

As the production comes to a close and the final curtain falls, Donella finds herself overcome with a mix of emotions. The audience's applause echoes in her ears as she takes her final bow, a sense of accomplishment washing over her. But amidst the excitement and celebration, there's also a bittersweet nostalgia and recognition that this chapter of her journey is ending.

Donella: (Taking a deep breath, her heart full) "It's hard to believe it's over. It feels like just yesterday we were starting rehearsals."

Co-star: (Approaching smiling) "You were incredible out there, Donella. I'm going to miss sharing the stage with you."

Donella: (Gratefully) "Thank you. It's been an amazing experience, hasn't it?"

As the cast gathers for one final celebration, Donella finds herself lost in thought, reflecting on the whirlwind of the past few months. She thinks back to the auditions, the late-night rehearsals, and the moments of camaraderie shared with her fellow actors.

Donella: (Looking around at her friends and colleagues, a sense of gratitude welled inside her) "I couldn't have asked for a better group of people to share this journey with."

Director: (Approaching with a smile) "Donella, you were a true standout in this production. Your talent and dedication shone through in every performance."

Donella: (Humbling) "Thank you, Director. It means the world to me."

. . .

As the night wears on and the celebration winds down, Donella finds herself alone with her thoughts, the quiet of the theatre enveloping her like a comforting embrace. She takes a moment to savor the stillness, letting the memories of the production wash over her.

Donella: (Reflecting on her journey so far) "It's been a whirlwind, that's for sure. But every moment and every challenge has been worth it. I've grown so much as an actor and as a person."

With a sense of closure and gratitude, Donella takes one last look around the empty theatre, committing the moment to memory. She knows this production may be over, but her journey is far from finished. There are new roles to tackle, challenges to over-come, and dreams to chase.

Donella: (Looking ahead with determination) "Here's to the next adventure. I can't wait to see what the future holds."

As she enters the night, the stars twinkling overhead, Donella feels a sense of anticipation building within her. The world is vast and full of possibilities, and she's ready to embrace them all.

Donella: (Whispering to herself) "This is just the beginning."

With a renewed purpose and a heart full of hope, Donella sets off into the night, ready to chase her dreams wherever they lead.

Chapter Five

NEW HORIZONS

As dawn breaks over the horizon, Donella wakes with an excitement bubbling within her. Today marks the beginning of a new chapter in her journey, a chance to explore new horizons and chase new dreams.

Donella: (Stretching, a smile playing on her lips) "Today is the day."

With a quick breakfast and a heart full of anticipation, Donella sets out into the bustling streets of her hometown. Her destination? The local travel agency is where she's set to embark on an adventure unlike any she's experienced.

· · ·

The travel agency is a hive of activity filled with travelers eager to explore the world beyond their doorstep. Donella waits patiently in line, her mind buzzing about the journey ahead.

Travel Agent: (Greeting her with a warm smile) "Good morning! How can I assist you today?"

Donella: (Beaming) "I'm looking to book a trip. Somewhere far away, somewhere I've never been before."

With the travel agent's help, Donella selects a destination that speaks to her sense of adventure, a vibrant city teeming with culture, art, and opportunity.

Donella: (Excitedly) "That's perfect. When do I leave?"

Travel Agent: (Checking the availability) "We have a flight leaving tomorrow morning. Does that work for you?"

. . .

Donella: (Nodding eagerly) "Absolutely. Book it."

With her flight booked and her bags packed, Donella spends the rest of the day tying up loose ends and saying farewells to friends and family.

Donella's Mother: (Hugging her tightly) "I'm going to miss you, my dear. But I'm so proud of you for following your dreams."

Donella's Father: (Clasping her hand) "Remember, no matter where you go, you'll always have a home here."

As the sun sets on her final night at home, Donella feels a mix of emotions swirling within her: excitement, anticipation, and a twinge of sadness at leaving behind the familiar comforts of home. But deep down, she knows this is exactly where she's meant to be in pursuing her dreams, wherever they may lead.

Donella: (Looking out at the starlit sky, a sense of peace washing over her) "This is it. The beginning of a new adventure."

. . .

And as she drifts off to sleep, the promise of tomorrow hangs in the air, a promise of new experiences, new challenges, and new horizons waiting to be explored.

Chapter Six

A CHANGE OF COURSE

As Donella stood outside the bustling airport terminal, her phone buzzed in her hand. She quickly glanced at the caller ID and saw it was an unfamiliar number. Curious, she answered the call, not expecting the life-changing news that awaited her on the other end.

Donella: (Answering the call, her heart pounding with anticipation) "Hello?"

Cruise Line Representative: (Excitedly) "Hi, Donella! It's [Name] from the cruise line. I'm calling to offer you the Entertainment Director's Assistant position on board our ship!

· · ·

Donella's breath caught in her throat as she processed the words. She had been dreaming of this opportunity, a chance to embark on a new adventure and pursue her passion for entertainment on the high seas.

Donella: (Overwhelmed with emotion) "Thank you so much! I'm beyond excited for this opportunity."

With her heart racing and excitement coursing through her veins, Donella quickly realized that her plans were about to change. Instead of heading to Hawaii, she would now set sail for a new destination, a career on board a cruise ship.

Donella: (Calling the airline to change her flight, her voice filled with excitement) "Hi, I need to change my flight. I've just been offered a job on a cruise ship, and I need to get to the training location as soon as possible."

After a flurry of phone calls and rearranged plans, Donella found herself with a new flight itinerary and a sense of anticipation for the journey ahead. She would have to wait two more days before she could fly, but the wait only added to her excitement.

Donella: (Talking to her mentor, her voice filled with gratitude) "Boss, I can't believe this is happening. Thank you for believing in me and giving me this opportunity."

Unbeknownst to Donella, her mentor had played a pivotal role in securing the job for her, filling out forms and pulling strings behind the scenes. His support and belief in her abilities had opened doors she never thought possible.

Donella: (Reflecting on the turn of events, her voice filled with wonder) "Everything is falling into place, just like you said it would. I can't wait to see where this journey takes me."

With her bags packed and her dreams within reach, Donella set off for the airport again, ready to embark on a new adventure and embrace the opportunities ahead.

. . .

Donella: (Looking out at the horizon, her eyes alight with excitement) "Here's to new beginnings and the endless possibilities that await."

As the plane taxied down the runway, Donella felt a sense of exhilaration wash over her. She was heading towards her new destination with a heart full of hope and a spirit ready to soar.

Chapter Seven

SEIZING OPPORTUNITIES

As Donella's parents drove her to the airport, her mother's tearful goodbyes mingled with words of encouragement and pride.

Mother: (Tears glistening in her eyes) "We'll miss you so much, my dear. But we're so proud of you for chasing your dreams."

Donella: (Smiling through her tears) "Thank you, Mom. I'll call you as soon as I can."

Arriving at the airport, Donella approached the boarding pass attendant, her excitement palpable as she handed over her ticket.

. . .

Attendant: (Warmly) "Welcome aboard, Miss Donella. We're thrilled to have you with us today."

With a final wave to her parents, Donella passed through security and boarded the plane, the hum of the engines signaling the start of her new adventure.

The flight was a whirlwind of excitement and anticipation, with Donella's thoughts racing ahead to the training that awaited her in Boston. She couldn't wait to dive into the entertainment world and learn everything she could about her new role.

Upon landing, Donella had a brief layover before catching her connecting flight to Boston. As she settled into her seat, she couldn't help but marvel at the journey ahead—a week of intensive training followed by a career on the Caribbean cruise line.

With each passing mile, Donella felt the excitement building within her. She was heading towards her new destination with a heart full of hope and a spirit ready to embrace whatever challenges lay ahead.

As the plane touched down in Boston, Donella felt the excitement wash over her. The city was bustling with energy and possibility, and she couldn't wait to explore everything it offered.

Stepping off the plane, Donella took a deep breath, ready to embark on the next chapter of her journey. With determination and anticipation, she set off into the bustling terminal, eager to begin her training and start her new career.

As Donella stepped off the plane in Boston, she was greeted by the hustle and bustle of the airport terminal. The air was alive with excitement and anticipation, mirroring the emotions coursing through her veins.

She followed the signs to the baggage claim area, her eyes scanning the crowd for any familiar faces. Despite being in a new city, she felt comfort knowing she was one step closer to her dream.

As she waited for her luggage to arrive, Donella couldn't help but reflect on the journey that had brought her here. From her humble beginnings in Nigeria to this moment in a bustling airport halfway across the world, every step has led her closer to her passion for entertainment.

The carousel whirred to life, and Donella's heart skipped a beat as she spotted her suitcase approaching her. She grabbed her bag and approached the exit with purpose, eager to start her training.

Outside the airport, Donella hailed a taxi and gave the driver the address of her hotel. As they weaved through the streets of Boston, she couldn't help but marvel at the sights and sounds of the city.

Arriving at her hotel, Donella was greeted by the receptionist's warm smile.

Receptionist: (Friendly) "Welcome to Boston, Miss Donella. I hope you enjoy your stay with us."

. . .

Donella: (Gratefully) "Thank you. I'm looking forward to it."

As she settled into her room, Donella continued with the excitement building within her. Tomorrow would mark the beginning of her training, a week filled with learning, growth, and new experiences.

With a smile on her face and a heart full of hope, Donella drifted off to sleep, eager to see what the future held. Tomorrow was the start of something new, and she was ready to embrace it with open arms.

And so, as the night stretched on and the city of Boston buzzed with life, Donella slept soundly, dreaming of the adventures that awaited her on the high seas.

As Donella slept peacefully, her phone rang, jolting her awake. Rubbing the sleep from her eyes, she answered to find her mentor's comforting voice on the other end.

Donella: (Groggy) "Hello?"

. . .

Mentor: (Warmly) "Donella, it's me. I just wanted to make sure you arrived safely."

Donella: (Gratefully) "Yes, sir. I made it to Boston just fine."

Mentor: (Reassuringly) "That's great to hear. Tomorrow morning, a van will be waiting for you outside your hotel to take you to the training facility. Others will be in the lobby, so just follow the signs, and they'll call your name."

Donella: (Relieved) "Thank you, sir. I appreciate you always looking out for me, especially in a place where I don't know anyone. Your voice brings me comfort."

Mentor: (Kindly) "You've got this, Donella. I believe in you. Now get some rest and prepare for tomorrow. It's the start of something incredible."

With her mentor's words echoing in her mind, Donella drifted back to sleep, feeling reassurance and confidence invade her.

The following day, Donella woke with renewed determination. After a quick breakfast, she made her way to the lobby, where a group of people had already gathered, each filled with anticipation for the day ahead.

As she waited for the van to arrive, Donella struck up conversations with her fellow trainees, exchanging stories and sharing in the excitement of the journey they were about to embark on.

Soon enough, the van pulled outside the hotel, and Donella joined the others as they piled in, eager to begin the next chapter of their adventure.

The ride to the training facility was filled with chatter and laughter as the group bonded over their excitement and nerves. Donella appreciated the camaraderie with her fellow trainees, knowing they were all in this together.

. . .

As they arrived at the facility, Donella's heart raced with anticipation. This was where her journey would genuinely begin—a week of intensive training that would prepare her for the challenges and excitement of life on board a cruise ship.

With a deep breath and determination, Donella stepped out of the van and into the unknown, ready to embrace whatever lay ahead.

As the group arrived at the training facility, they were greeted by Mr. Johnson, their director, for the next seven days. He exuded an air of authority and confidence, instantly commanding the attention of everyone present.

Mr. Johnson: (Addressing the group with a warm smile) "Good morning, everyone. My name is Mr. Johnson, and I'll be your director for the duration of your training. Welcome aboard!"

His voice was firm yet friendly, instilling a sense of trust and respect in his audience. Donella was drawn to his presence, reassured by the knowledge that they were in capable hands.

. . .

Mr. Johnson led the group inside the facility, where rows of chairs were set up in a spacious classroom. Posters adorned the walls, displaying essential safety procedures and emergency protocols.

Mr. Johnson: (Gesturing to the classroom) "This will be our home base for the next week. Here, we'll cover everything you need to know to ensure the safety and well-being of both you and the passengers on board."

With Mr. Johnson at the helm, the training sessions were thorough and informative. He guided the group through each course with patience and expertise, ensuring they understood the importance of their role on board a cruise ship.

During breaks, Mr. Johnson took the time to get to know each trainee individually, offering words of encouragement and support.

Mr. Johnson: (Approaching Donella with a smile) "Donella, I've heard great things about you. Keep up the good work. You're going to go far in this industry."

Donella felt a surge of confidence knowing that she had Mr. Johnson's support and guidance every step of the way. With his leadership, she knew she was prepared to tackle challenges.

As the week progressed, Donella and her fellow trainees immersed themselves in their studies, soaking up every piece of knowledge Mr. Johnson imparted. From emergency evacuation procedures to guest services etiquette, they absorbed it all with enthusiasm and determination.

Mr. Johnson gathered the group for a special announcement on the final training day.

Mr. Johnson: (Addressing the trainees with pride) "Congratulations, everyone. You've successfully completed all six vital courses, and I'm pleased to say that you are now certified to work on any cruise ship."

. . .

A round of applause filled the room as the trainees celebrated their accomplishment. Donella felt a swell of pride in her chest, knowing she was one step closer to her dream of working on the high seas.

With a handshake and a smile, Mr. Johnson handed each trainee their Certificate of Completion, marking the end of their training and the beginning of their careers.

As Donella held her certificate in her hands, she couldn't help but feel excitement for the adventures that lay ahead. With Mr. Johnson's guidance and support, she was ready to set sail and embrace the journey that awaited her.

As Donella spoke to her mother over the phone, her voice filled with excitement and pride as she recounted the past week's events. She described the intense training exercises, including the simulation of a burning building filled with smoke, where she had to navigate through the darkness and chaos to rescue passengers.

· · ·

Donella: (Excitedly) "Mom, you wouldn't believe it! We had to go into this burning building, full of smoke, and carry dummies out to safety. It was intense, but I managed to find my way through and make it out in time."

Her mother listened intently, her heart swelling with pride for her daughter's bravery and determination.

Mother: (Reassuringly) "That's my girl. I always knew you were capable of anything you set your mind to."

Donella continued to recount her experiences, including the rigorous drills they had to undergo to prepare for emergencies at sea. She explained how they had to practice boarding a dinghy and rescuing passengers from the water, all while maintaining calm and composure under pressure.

Donella: (Excitedly) "And then, Mom, we had to practice getting into a dinghy and rescuing people from the water. It was challenging, but I managed to stay focused and help others in need."

. . .

As Donella spoke, her parents listened with a mixture of awe and pride, amazed by their daughter's courage and determination.

Father: (Gratefully) "We're so proud of you, Donella. You've worked hard to get where you are, and it's all paying off."

Donella smiled, appreciating how gratitude washed over her. She knew that none of this would have been possible without the unwavering support of her parents and her mentor, who had believed in her every step of the way.

Donella: (Gratefully) "Thank you, Mom and Dad. I couldn't have done it without you. And guess what? I just found out I have an appointment to get my International Visa. It's all coming together, just like we hoped."

As she hung up the phone, Donella felt excitement and anticipation for the journey ahead. With her training complete and her visa in hand, she was ready to embark on her first cruise and begin the next chapter of her adventure.

Chapter Eight

A NEW CHAPTER

As Donella boards the cruise ship, she is greeted by a representative from the entertainment department.

Entertainment Representative: "Welcome aboard, Donella! We're thrilled to have you join us."

Donella: "Thank you so much! I'm beyond excited to be here."

As they make their way to meet the Entertainment Director, Donella takes in the grandeur of the ship and the bustling atmosphere of the onboard entertainment venues.

. . .

Entertainment Representative: "Donella, meet Mr. Thompson, our Entertainment Director."

Mr. Thompson: (Extending his hand with a warm smile) "Welcome, Donella. We're delighted to have you join our team."

Donella: (Shaking his hand eagerly) "Thank you, Mr. Thompson. I'm honored to be here and eager to learn everything I can."

As Donella settles into her new role, she collaborates with her colleagues to plan and execute various entertainment events and performances.

Colleague: "Donella, we're counting on you to help make tonight's show successful."

Donella: "You can count on me. Let's make it unforgettable!"

. . .

Donella works tirelessly with her new colleagues to bring joy and excitement to passengers aboard the cruise ship, embracing her new role with passion and determination.

Several days into her new role on the cruise ship, Donella takes a moment to call her longtime mentor, addressing him respectfully as always.

Donella: (Dialing her mentor's number with anticipation) "Hello, sir, it's Donella. How are you today?"

Mentor: (Warmly) "Donella, it's wonderful to hear from you. I'm doing well, thank you. And yourself?"

Donella: (With a hint of excitement) "I'm doing great, sir. I just had to call and tell you all about my new position. I'm an entertainment director's assistant on a cruise ship!"

Mentor: (Pleased) "That sounds like an incredible opportunity, Donella. I'm proud of you for seizing it."

· · ·

Donella: (Gratefully) "Thank you, sir. I couldn't have done it without your guidance and support over the years."

Mentor: (Encouragingly) "You've always had the talent and determination, Donella. I'm glad to see you thriving."

Donella: (Eagerly sharing her experiences) "It's been an amazing experience so far, sir. The atmosphere on the ship, the team's creativity—it's truly inspiring."

Mentor: (Proudly) "I knew you would excel in such an environment, Donella. Keep up the excellent work."

Donella: (Determined) "I will, sir. Thank you for always believing in me."

Mentor: (Warmly) "It's been my pleasure, Donella. Remember, the sky's the limit for you."

·   ·   ·

Donella: (Filled with determination) "Yes, sir. I won't let you down."

With the encouragement of her mentor ringing in her ears, Donella returns to her duties on the cruise ship, ready to continue making her mark in the world of entertainment.

As Donella reminisces about her mentor's guidance, she can't help but recall the countless conversations they shared on WhatsApp, discussing her dreams and aspirations.

Donella: (Reflecting fondly) "Sir, do you remember all those late-night chats we had on WhatsApp? You were always there to listen to my hopes and fears, guiding me through every decision."

Mentor: (Nostalgically) "Of course, Donella. Those conversations meant a lot to me as well. It was a privilege to be a part of your journey."

·   ·   ·

Donella recalls the numerous times she filled out applications and forms, each a small step toward her goal of working on a cruise ship and experiencing a new life.

Donella: (Thoughtfully) "Sir, do you remember how many times I filled out those applications to work on a cruise ship? It felt like I was constantly sending them out, hoping for a chance to leave behind everything and start fresh."

Mentor: (Encouragingly) "I remember, Donella. Your determination and perseverance were truly admirable. You never gave up on your dreams, no matter how many obstacles stood in your way."

With gratitude for her mentor's unwavering support and encouragement, Donella reflects on the journey that brought her to where she is today.

Donella: (Gratefully) "Thank you, sir, for always believing in me and pushing me to pursue my dreams. I wouldn't be here without you."

. . .

Mentor: (Proudly) "You've come a long way, Donella. I do not doubt you'll continue to achieve great things in your career and beyond."

With her mentor's words echoing in her mind, Donella feels a renewed determination to make the most of her opportunity on the cruise ship and embrace the new life that awaits her.

Donella: "Sir, remember when we talked about starting an online store together? It was just an idea back then, but look at it now: it's become a thriving business specializing in fashion."

Mentor: "Indeed, Donella. I remember those conversations vividly. It's incredible to see how far you've come with the online store. Your dedication and hard work have truly paid off."

Donella: "Thank you, sir. The store not only helped support my family but also provided opportunities for my brothers. They've been able to pursue their dreams, just likc I have."

. . .

Mentor: "That's wonderful to hear, Donella. It's a testament to your entrepreneurial spirit and determination to succeed. Your success is not just your own. It's a reflection of the support and love of your family."

Donella: "Absolutely, sir. I'm grateful for their support every step of the way. And now, with this opportunity on the cruise ship, I hope to continue making them proud and giving back to them as much as they've given to me."

Mentor: "I have no doubt you will, Donella. Your resilience and drive have always been inspiring. Keep pushing forward, and remember that I'm here cheering you on every step of the way."

Donella: "Thank you, sir. Your mentorship has been invaluable to me, and I'll always be grateful for your guidance and support."

With renewed purpose and gratitude for her mentor's unwavering support, Donella looks forward to the future and is ready to embrace the challenges and opportunities.

. . .

As Donella reflects on her journey, she feels fulfillment knowing that she has overcome obstacles and achieved her dreams with the support of her mentor. With a heart impregnated with gratitude, she looks ahead to the future with anticipation and excitement.

Donella: (Contemplatively) "It's been quite a journey, hasn't it, sir? From uncertain beginnings to realizing my dreams, I've come a long way."

Mentor: (Proudly) "Indeed, Donella. I've watched you grow and flourish into the remarkable person you are today. Your journey is an inspiration to us all."

Donella: (Determined) "Now, I want to pay it forward and become a mentor to someone else, guiding them on their path to success and fulfillment."

Mentor: (Encouragingly) "That's a noble goal, Donella. Your experiences and wisdom will undoubtedly make a positive impact on those you mentor.”

Donella: (With a smile) “I look forward to the opportunity to help someone else discover their passion and reach their full potential, just as you did for me, sir.”

Mentor: (Warmly) “I do not doubt that you will make an exceptional mentor, Donella. Your journey has equipped you with the insight and empathy needed to guide others toward their destiny.”

As Donella prepares for her new role as a mentor, she embraces the future with optimism and determination, ready to inspire and empower others to pursue their dreams with unwavering courage and resilience.

Chapter Nine

FORBIDDEN LOVE

As the days turned into weeks and the weeks into months, Donella grew increasingly attached to her mentor. What had started as a professional relationship had blossomed into something more profound, a bond forged through late-night conversations and shared dreams?

Donella: (Voice trembling with emotion) "I have to tell you something, sir. I've come to realize that I... I love you."

Her words hung heavy in the air, a confession she had held onto for far too long. But as soon as the words left her lips, Donella felt a surge of panic wash over her. What had she done?

Mentor: (Voice gentle, yet pained) "Donella, you know I care for you deeply. But we both know that this... this is not right. I'm married, and there's a significant age difference between us. We can't... we can't pursue this any further."

Donella's heart sank at his words, a painful realization settling in her chest. She had known deep down that their love was forbidden, but she couldn't deny the feelings that had grown between them.

Mentor: (Voice filled with regret) "I wish things were different, Donella. I wish I could show you how much you mean to me. But I can't. We have to maintain the boundaries of our relationship."

Despite the ache in her heart, Donella knew her mentor was right. Their love was a flame that could never be fully ignited, a passion that would only lead to pain and heartache for them both.

Donella: (Voice barely above a whisper) "I understand, sir. I'm sorry for putting you in this position."

With a heavy heart, Donella vowed to bury her feelings deep within her soul, to lock them away where they could no longer cause harm. But she knew that her love for her mentor would never truly fade. It would linger in the shadows, a constant reminder of what could never be.

As the days passed, Donella and her mentor continued their conversations, their bond stronger than ever. But beneath the surface was sadness and a longing for love that could never be realized.

And so, as they navigated the complexities of their relationship, Donella let herself wonder what might have been if only their love had been allowed to flourish. But in the end, she knew that some loves were not meant to be.

As the ship docked in Hawaii, Donella sensed a feeling of anticipation building within her. Three weeks of vacation awaited her on the mainland, and she couldn't wait to explore all the beautiful islands had to offer. With her time off, she decided to treat herself to a stay at a luxurious hotel where she could unwind and indulge in much-needed relaxation.

Donella: (Dialing the phone with excitement) "Hello, sir? It's Donella. I wanted to let you know that I'll have some time off the ship and would love for you to join me. Would you be interested?"

Her heart raced as she waited for his response, hoping against hope that he would agree to spend this special time with her.

Mentor: (Warmly) "Donella, I'm deeply honored by your invitation. I would be delighted to join you for your vacation. Let's make it unforgettable."

With plans in place and excitement building, Donella couldn't help but feel a flutter of anticipation in her stomach. This vacation was exactly what she needed: a chance to escape the confines of the ship and spend quality time with the man she admired and respected so much.

. . .

As the clock struck midnight, Donella found herself sitting at the bedside of her hotel room, the soft glow of the moon casting a gentle light across the room. With trembling fingers, she picked up the phone and dialed her mentor's number, her heart pounding excitedly.

Mentor: (Answering the phone, his voice filled with warmth) "Donella, is that you?"

Donella: (Smiling softly) "Yes, it's me. I just wanted to hear your voice before we embark on this adventure together."

Their conversation flowed effortlessly, each word strengthening the bond between them. Despite the professional boundaries that had always existed between them, Donella felt closer to her mentor than ever before.

As they spoke into the early morning hours, Donella couldn't shake the feeling that this vacation would be the beginning of something extraordinary. With her mentor by her side, she knew the days ahead would be filled with laughter, discovery, and perhaps even a hint of romance.

As she finally drifted off to sleep, a wave of contentment washed over her, knowing she had found a companion who understood her in a way no one else ever could.

As the days unfolded on the beautiful island of Hawaii, Donella and her mentor immersed themselves in a world of adventure and discovery. They explored the lush landscapes, hiked through tropical forests, and basked in the sun's warm glow as they lounged on pristine beaches.

Their bond grew stronger each day, fueled by shared experiences and mutual respect. They laughed, shared stories, and marveled at the world's beauty.

Donella: (Smiling as they walk along the beach) "I never imagined I'd be spending my vacation like this with you, exploring paradise."

· · ·

Mentor: (Gratefully) "It's moments like these that make life truly special. I'm grateful for the opportunity to share them with you, Donella."

Despite their undeniable chemistry, Donella and her mentor remained steadfast in their commitment to maintaining professional boundaries. They knew that any romantic involvement would only complicate their relationship and potentially jeopardize the trust and respect they had worked so hard to build.

Donella: (Reflectively) "It's strange, isn't it? How easily could we cross that line, but we choose not to? It's a testament to the strength of our connection and the respect we have for each other."

Mentor: (Nodding in agreement) "Absolutely. Our friendship means everything to me, and I wouldn't do anything to jeopardize it."

As the sun set on their final evening in Hawaii, Donella and her mentor sat side by side, watching the colors of the sky shift and change in the fading light. In that moment, they knew their bond was stronger than any fleeting romance built on a foundation of trust, understanding, and unwavering support.

Donella: (Softly) "Thank you for being here with me and for sharing this experience with me."

Mentor: (Sincerely) "Thank you, Donella. For everything."

As they embraced the beauty of the moment, Donella and her mentor realized that sometimes the most powerful connections are the ones that defy expectations, transcending the boundaries of time and circumstance. And as they prepared to return to the ship, they knew their friendship would continue to flourish, unburdened by the weight of what could have been.

Donella and her mentor shared a moment of quiet intimacy as they sat on the soft, luscious couch in the dimly lit lounge, overlooking the vast expanse of the ocean shimmering under the moonlight. The gentle sound of the waves crashing against the shore filled the air, adding to the romantic ambiance of the evening.

. . .

Donella: (Contentedly) "It's so peaceful here, isn't it?"

Mentor: (Softly) "Yes, it is. There's something about the ocean at night that feels... magical."

As the night stretched on, Donella nestled her head in her mentor's lap, feeling the warmth of his touch and the steady rhythm of his breathing. He gently stroked her hair, his touch sending shivers down her spine.

Mentor: (Tenderly) "You know, Donella, I cherish moments like these. Just being here with you, in this moment, feels like... everything."

Donella: (Sighing softly) "Me too. It's moments like these that make me grateful for everything we have."

Their hearts beat in sync as they gazed out at the moonlit ocean, lost in the beauty of the night and the comfort of each other's presence. At that moment, there were no boundaries, no obligations, just two souls connecting in the quiet stillness of the night.

They remained embraced as the hours passed, savoring every moment together. As the first light of dawn began to creep over the horizon, Donella knew that this night would be etched in her memory forever, a reminder of the love and connection they shared despite the challenges ahead.

As the elevator ascended to the 20th floor, Donella and her mentor stood side by side, their hands intertwined in a silent acknowledgment of the unspoken desire between them. With each passing floor, the tension in the air grew palpable, anticipation building with every heartbeat.

Donella: (Voice barely above a whisper) "This is it."

Mentor: (Nodding, his voice husky with emotion) "Yes, it is."

. . .

As the elevator doors slid open on the 20th floor, Donella held her mentor's hand firmly, silently urging him to stay with her. They lingered on the threshold momentarily, their eyes locked in a silent exchange of longing and desire.

But as the elevator doors began to close, Donella made a split-second decision. With a swift movement, she pulled her mentor into the elevator, the doors shutting behind them with a soft thud.

With each passing second, their hearts beat in unison, the space between them crackling with electricity. As the elevator ascended to the 23rd floor, Donella and her mentor remained locked in a passionate embrace, their lips meeting in a fervent kiss that ignited a fire within them both.

When the elevator finally reached their destination, they stepped out into the hallway, their hands still intertwined as they made their way to Donella's room. With each step, their connection deepened, their desire for one another burning brightly in the night.

. . .

As they crossed the threshold into Donella's room, they knew that this night would be one they would never forget a night of passion, love, and forbidden desire that would linger in their hearts long after the dawn broke on the horizon.

A bittersweet reality hung in the air as they sat together in the morning light, sharing breakfast in Donella's room. They both knew that what had transpired between them the night before was a moment of passion born out of a deep connection a love they could not deny but one that could never be fully realized.

Donella: (Quietly) "Thank you for breakfast, sir."

Mentor: (Softly) "You're welcome, Donella. It was the least I could do."

Their conversation was tinged with a melancholy undertone, a silent acknowledgment of the boundaries between them. And yet, amidst the sadness, there was also gratitude for the moments they had shared, for the love that had brought them together, if only for a fleeting moment.

. . .

As they finished their meal, Donella and her mentor rose from the table, their eyes meeting in a silent exchange of understanding. They knew that this was goodbye for now, at least.

Mentor: (Gently) "I should get going. My flight leaves soon."

Donella: (Nodding, her voice barely above a whisper) "Yes, of course."

They walked together to the door, their footsteps echoing in the quiet room. And as they stood in the hallway, their eyes locked in a final embrace, Donella felt a lump growing in her throat. She knew this was the end of their time together and forbidden love.

Mentor: (Softly) "I'll text you when I get home."

With a heavy heart, Donella nodded, her eyes brimming with unshed tears. She watched as her mentor disappeared down the hallway, his figure growing smaller and smaller until he was nothing more than a distant memory.

As she returned to the ship, Donella couldn't help but feel a deep emptiness wash over her. But amidst the pain, there was also a glimmer of hope a hope that someday, somehow, their paths would cross again, and they would find a way to love each other genuinely and adequately.

Chapter Ten

DEPARTURES AND REFLECTIONS

As Donella returned to the ship, her heart heavy with the weight of the night's farewell, she couldn't shake the emptiness settling in her chest. The hallway seemed to stretch endlessly as she returned to her cabin, the echoes of their final embrace still ringing in her ears.

Meanwhile, on the other side of the world, De mentor found himself boarding a flight to New York LaGuardia Airport. As he settled into his seat and gazed out the window, the vast ocean expanse stretched before him, a mosaic of islands and coastline disappearing into the horizon.

. . .

With each passing moment, De mentor's thoughts drifted back to his home, his wife, and the life he had left behind for this fleeting moment of freedom. He remembered the conversation they had shared before he left, her casual dismissal of his plans to take a vacation on his own.

"She didn't even wonder," he mused, a twinge of sadness tugging at his heart. "She knew it wasn't something I usually do, but she didn't protest. We've been together so long; she trusts me implicitly."

As the plane soared through the sky, De Mentor was overwhelmed by a pang of guilt gnawing at him. Despite his love for his wife and the life they had built together, part of him yearned for something different.

The scene outside his window shifted and changed with each passing moment, the landscape below transforming from endless ocean to sprawling cityscape as they approached New York. The sun cast long shadows across the skyscrapers, bathing the city in a golden glow.

· · ·

Anticipation grew inside De Mentor as the plane touched down at La Guardia Airport. He knew that the days ahead would be filled with uncertainty and possibility, a chance to explore a world beyond the confines of his everyday life.

But as he stepped off the plane and into the bustling terminal, De Mentor couldn't shake the feeling that he was leaving a part of himself behind. As he navigated the crowded corridors of the airport, he couldn't help but wonder what the future held in store for him at home and abroad.

Chapter Eleven

UNEXPECTED ENCOUNTERS

As the ship glided through the sparkling waters of the Caribbean, Donella found herself lost in a whirlwind of emotions. The memories of her time with her mentor still lingered in her mind, but she pushed them aside, focusing instead on the vibrant energy of the onboard entertainment scene.

Meanwhile, on another deck of the ship, De mentor walked hand in hand with his wife, their laughter mingling with the gentle hum of the ocean. It was a rare moment of tranquility for the couple, a chance to escape the hustle and bustle of everyday life and reconnect with each other.

· · ·

As they explored the ship's various activities and amenities, De mentor couldn't help but marvel at the beauty of the sea stretching out before them. It was a stark contrast to the concrete jungle of New York, a reminder of life's simple pleasures that often went unnoticed in the rush of modern-day living.

But amidst the excitement of their cruise, De mentor had the persistent feeling of deja vu that washed over him as he watched the onboard entertainment. And then, as fate would have it, he found himself drawn to one particular performance, a captivating showcase of talent that left him spellbound.

Donella's performance was nothing short of mesmerizing, her voice filling the air with a haunting melody that seemed to echo in the depths of his soul. As he watched her on stage, De mentor felt a connection he couldn't quite explain, a familiarity that tugged at his heartstrings and left him longing for more.

After the show, De mentor and his wife decided to grab a bitc to cat at one of the ship's many restaurants. And as luck would have it, they found themselves seated at a table next to none other than Donella herself.

The introductions were made, and soon, De mentor and Donella were engaged in lively conversation, their laughter mingling with the soft strains of music drifting through the air. It was as if they had known each other for years, their connection immediate and undeniable.

As the meal came to an end, De mentor couldn't ignore the feeling that this encounter was more than just a coincidence. There was something about Donella, something intangible yet unmistakable that drew him to her in a way he couldn't quite understand.

And then, as if reading his thoughts, Donella turned to him with a smile that lit up her face, her eyes sparkling with warmth and affection.

Donella: (Softly) "Thank you for joining us for lunch, De mentor. It's been a pleasure getting to know you."

. . .

De mand: (Gratefully) "The pleasure is all mine, Donella. There's something special about you, something that I can't quite put into words."

And at that moment, as they exchanged a meaningful glance, De mentor knew that this encounter was just the beginning of something beautiful, a connection that would endure, even in the vast expanse of the sea.

As Donella and the mentor, along with his wife, shared a warm embrace and exchanged heartfelt expressions of appreciation during their meal, they made a solemn vow to remain connected despite the distance. They pledged to keep in touch, knowing their bond transcended time and space.

As the mentor and his wife bid farewell and walked away, a tender moment of reflection passed between them. With a gentle smile, his wife inquired about the young lady he had been secretly supporting. With a nod and a twinkle in his eye, the mentor confirmed her suspicions, affirming that Donella indeed possessed the potential to shine brightly as a star.

Chapter Twelve

HOMECOMING AND MENTORSHIP

After four exhilarating tours at sea, Donella felt a pull towards home, a longing to reconnect with her roots and the people she held dear. As the ship docked at port, she bid farewell to her fellow crew members and stepped onto solid ground once more, her heart brimming with anticipation.

Returning home felt like stepping into a dream, a familiar landscape dotted with memories of childhood adventures and cherished moments with loved ones. Her hometown's sights, sounds, and smells enveloped her like a warm embrace, filling her with a sentiment of belonging that she had missed during her time at sea.

. . .

But amidst the joy of reunion, Donella felt a new purpose stirring within her a desire to give back to her community and make a difference in the lives of those in need. And so, she seized the opportunity to become a mentor to a young woman who shared her passion for the arts and dreams of a brighter future.

As she sat down with her mentee, Donella shared her journey of self-discovery and the lessons she had learned along the way. She listened intently as the young woman poured out her hopes, fears, and aspirations, offering guidance and support every step of the way.

Together, they embarked on a journey of growth and transformation, exploring new avenues of creativity and self-expression. Donella encouraged her mentee to embrace her talents and pursue her dreams with courage and determination, knowing that anything was possible with the proper guidance and support.

As the weeks turned into months, Donella watched with pride as her mentee blossomed into a confident and accomplished young woman, ready to take on the world with enthusiasm and determination. Their bond grew stronger each day, a testament to the power of mentorship and its impact on a person's life.

As Donella looked back on her journey from a small-town girl with big dreams to a seasoned entertainer and mentor, she felt a profound gratitude for the opportunities that had shaped her path. She knew that no matter where life took her next, she would always carry the lessons of love, resilience, and self-compassion, guiding her every step of the way.

Chapter Thirteen

HOMECOMING

Donella stepped off the bus onto the dusty streets of her hometown, feeling a rush of nostalgia wash over her as she took in the familiar sights and sounds. The air was filled with the scent of spices from nearby market stalls, and the sound of children playing echoed through the narrow alleyways.

As she made her way through the bustling marketplace, Donella couldn't help but smile at the sight of familiar faces. Old friends waved to her from across the street, and vendors greeted her with warm smiles as she passed by their stalls.

. . .

It wasn't long before Donella heard whispers of a young woman named Aisha, a local girl with dreams of seeing the world but unsure of how to make it a reality. Intrigued by Aisha's story, Donella felt a surge of empathy and determination to help her however she could.

After asking around, Donella learned that Aisha worked at a small cafe on the outskirts of town. Donella made her way to the cafe with a clear purpose, her heart pounding excitedly.

Upon arriving, Donella spotted Aisha behind the counter. Her face lit up with a bright smile as she greeted customers with warmth and enthusiasm. Donella approached her, introducing herself and explaining that she had heard about Aisha's dreams of traveling the world.

Aisha's eyes widened in surprise as she listened to Donella's words, her curiosity piqued by the stranger's sudden interest in her life. Sensing Aisha's hesitation, Donella reassured her that she wanted to offer guidance and support, having once been in a similar position.

. . .

After a moment of hesitation, Aisha nodded, her smile widening as she welcomed Donella's mentorship offer. With that, the two women sat down at a nearby table, their conversation filled with laughter and excitement as they discussed Aisha's dreams and aspirations for the future.

As the sun began to set over the horizon, Donella couldn't control the sensation of fulfillment washing over her. In Aisha, she saw a reflection of her younger self, a girl with dreams as vast as the open sky and a determination to chase them no matter the obstacles in her path. As they parted ways that evening, Donella knew she had found a kindred spirit in Aisha, someone whose journey she was eager to support and witness unfolded.

As the evening wore on, Donella and Aisha delved deeper into their conversation, sharing stories of their respective journeys and the obstacles they had overcome along the way. Donella admired Aisha's resilience and determination, seeing in her a spark of potential that reminded her of her own aspirations when she was younger.

· · ·

Donella was inevitably struck by Aisha's beauty and grace, her dark eyes shining with hope and uncertainty. Despite her outward confidence, Donella acknowledged Aisha's vulnerability, fear of the unknown, and longing for guidance and support.

Sitting across from Aisha, Donella felt an inexplicable surge of compassion and empathy towards the young woman before her. She saw herself reflected in Aisha's eyes—a girl with dreams as vast as the open sky, yet unsure how to navigate the path ahead.

As they continued talking, Donella shared stories of her experiences traveling the world and pursuing her dreams. She spoke of the challenges she had faced and the lessons she had learned.

Chapter Fourteen

A NEW CONNECTION

ate at night, as the world outside grew quiet and still, Donella found herself sitting at her desk, her laptop screen illuminating the dimly lit room. With a cup of tea in hand, she opened a chat window and began typing out a message to her mentor, her thoughts filled with excitement and anticipation.

"Hello, sir," Donella wrote, her fingers flying across the keyboard. "I hope you're doing well. I wanted to tell you about someone I met recently, a young woman named Aisha. She dreams of becoming a flight attendant and traveling the world, but she's unsure where to start. I see so much potential in her, and I want to help her however I can."

. . .

Donella was delighted as she hit send, knowing she was taking the first steps towards helping Aisha achieve her dreams. She knew her mentor would understand and support her decision, as he always had.

Sure enough, a few moments later, her mentor's reply came through, filled with words of encouragement and wisdom.

"Donella, I'm proud of you for taking the initiative to help someone in need. Remember, your time and attention are the greatest gifts you can give someone. By sharing your own experiences and offering guidance, you have the power to change someone's life for the better. Keep up the good work, and never underestimate the impact you can have on those around you."

Donella smiled as she read her mentor's words and experienced a renewed sense of purpose and determination coursing through her veins. She knew she had found a kindred spirit in Aisha, a young woman with dreams as big as the sky, just waiting to take flight.

· · ·

With her mentor's words echoing in her mind, Donella returned to her conversation with Aisha, eager to continue guiding and supporting her on the journey ahead. Together, they would chart a course toward a future filled with endless possibilities and boundless opportunities, one small step at a time.

Chapter Fifteen

SETTING GOALS

As Donella and Aisha sat down together to discuss Aisha's career aspirations, Donella couldn't contain a surge of excitement at the prospect of helping Aisha turn her dreams into reality. She knew setting specific, achievable goals would be the first step toward success.

"All right, Aisha," Donella began, her voice filled with enthusiasm. "Let's start by outlining your goals for your aviation career. What exactly do you hope to achieve?"

Aisha took a moment to gather her thoughts before responding, her eyes shining with determination. "I want to become a flight attendant and travel the world," she said firmly. "I want to see new places, meet new people, and experience different cultures."

"Fantastic," Donella exclaimed, nodding in approval. "Now, let's break down those goals into smaller, more manageable steps. First, we need to consider the qualifications and skills required to become a flight attendant."

Donella and Aisha discussed the necessary requirements, including customer service experience, language proficiency, and safety training. Donella encouraged Aisha to assess her current skill set and identify areas where she may need to improve or gain new skills.

"Aside from your current job at the cafe, do you have any other experience in customer service?" Donella asked, eager to help Aisha build a strong foundation for her future career.

Aisha shook her head; her brow furrowed in thought. "No, not really," she admitted. "But I'm a quick learner, and I'm willing to put in the effort to gain the necessary experience."

· · ·

"That's the spirit," Donella replied, smiling encouragingly. "We can start by seeking opportunities to gain customer service experience, whether through volunteer work, part-time jobs, or even online courses."

As their conversation continued, Donella's mentor contacted her via chat, asking about her family and how her brothers were doing. Donella paused momentarily, her thoughts turning to her brother, a bright, ambitious young man with their dreams.

"They're doing well, sir," Donella replied, typing her response. "One of them is studying to be a scientist, and the other is pursuing a career in engineering. They're both working hard to achieve their goals, just like I am."

Her mentor's response was swift and filled with pride. "I'm glad to hear that, Donella. It sounds like your family is full of ambitious individuals with bright futures ahead of them. Keep supporting each other and chasing your dreams. I do not doubt that you'll all achieve great things."

. . .

Filled with a fresh determination, Donella turned her attention back to Aisha, eager to continue guiding her toward a future filled with endless possibilities and opportunities. Together, they would embark on a journey of self-discovery and personal growth, one step at a time.

TAKING ACTIONS

With Donella's guidance, Aisha wasted no time taking proactive steps towards becoming a flight attendant. Armed with renewed determination and a clear action plan, she dived headfirst into preparing for her future career.

The first order of business was updating her resume to highlight her relevant skills and experiences. With Donella's help, Aisha carefully crafted a polished resume that showcased her customer service skills, language proficiency, and commitment to excellence. Donella provided valuable feedback and suggestions, ensuring Aisha's resume stood out to potential employers.

. . .

Next, they focused on practicing interview techniques to help Aisha feel confident and prepared for the rigorous selection process. Together, they conducted mock interviews, role-playing various scenarios and questions commonly asked during flight attendant interviews. Donella offered constructive criticism and encouragement, helping Aisha refine her responses and presentation skills.

With her resume revamped and her interview skills honed, Aisha wasted no time applying for entry-level positions in the airline industry. Donella encouraged her to cast a wide net and explore opportunities with different airlines, emphasizing the importance of persistence and resilience in the face of rejection.

"Don't be discouraged by setbacks," Donella reminded Aisha, her voice filled with unwavering support. "Every rejection is a learning opportunity that brings you one step closer to success. Keep pushing forward, and never lose sight of your dreams."

As the evening drew to a close, Donella reached for her phone, her fingers hovering over the familiar number she had dialed countless times before. With a deep breath, she pressed the call button, her heart racing with anticipation.

"Hello, sir," Donella greeted her mentor warmly, her voice filled with genuine affection. "I just wanted to check in and see how you're doing. How's your mom? How's your wife? Is everything good on your end?"

Her mentor's response was filled with warmth and gratitude as he shared updates on his family and expressed his appreciation for Donella's continued support and friendship. As they exchanged pleasantries and caught up on each other's lives, Donella was inevitably filled with gratitude for the mentorship and guidance she had received along her journey.

With revitalized determination and a deep sense of purpose, Donella knew that she and Aisha were well on their way to achieving their dreams, one step at a time. And with her mentor beside her, she felt confident that anything was possible.

A bittersweet feeling settled over her as Donella prepared to leave home once again and return to the cruise ship. She knew she had a challenging journey ahead of her, with four back-to-back tours awaiting her on the ship. Saying goodbye to her family was never easy, but this time felt especially poignant as she knew she would be away for about a year.

Her family gathered around her, their faces filled with pride and love, as they bid her farewell. They had thrown a small party in her honor, with laughter and music filling the air as they celebrated her accomplishments and wished her well on her journey.

Donella hugged each of them tightly, her heart overflowing with love and gratitude for the unwavering support they had shown her throughout her life. She kissed her parents on the cheek, whispered words of love and encouragement to her brothers, and promised to stay in touch as often as possible.

Even the local man production company members, who had become like a second family to her, came to visit her before she left. They shared memories and laughter, reminiscing about the productions they had worked on together and the bonds they had formed along the way.

$$\cdot \quad \cdot \quad \cdot$$

As the time came for Donella to board the ship and begin her journey, she felt a mix of emotions swirling inside her: excitement for the adventures that awaited her, sadness at leaving her loved ones behind, and gratitude for the opportunities that awaited.

With one last wave to her family and friends, Donella stepped onto the plane, her heart filled with hope and determination. She knew this was just the beginning of her journey, and she was ready to embrace whatever challenges and triumphs lay ahead with courage and grace. As the plane lifted towards new horizons, Donella looked towards the future with optimism and excitement, knowing she was precisely where she was meant to be.

Chapter Seventeen

ACHEIVING SUCCESS

After weeks of hard work and determination, Aisha's perseverance pays off as she receives an offer to join a prestigious airline as a flight attendant. Overwhelmed with joy and gratitude, she can hardly contain her excitement as she shares the news with Donella, her voice trembling with emotion.

"Donella, I got the job!" Aisha exclaims, her words bursting with happiness. "I can't believe it! I'm going to be a flight attendant!"

Donella's heart swells with pride as she listens to Aisha's words, knowing that her efforts and guidance have played a significant role in Aisha's success. She congratulates Aisha warmly, her voice filled with genuine happiness for her friend's achievement.

"I knew you could do it, Aisha," Donella replies, her voice filled with pride. "You worked so hard and never gave up, and now you're reaping the rewards of your perseverance. I couldn't be happier for you."

As Aisha prepares to embark on her new career journey, she looks to Donella as a mentor and role model, grateful for the invaluable lessons she has learned along the way. She asks Donella how she can repay her for her unwavering support and guidance.

"Don't worry about repaying me, Aisha," Donella replies, her voice filled with warmth. "The best way you can thank me is by paying it forward, just as I passed on kindness from my mentor to you. Help someone who needs guidance and support, and continue spreading kindness wherever you go."

With a restored sense of purpose and gratitude, Aisha promises to do just that, eager to share the lessons she has learned and the support she has received with others who may be on a similar journey.

After she hangs up the phone with Aisha, Donella takes a moment to reflect on the impact of her actions. She knows that she has made a difference in Aisha's life, just as her mentor had made a difference in hers. As she gazes out at the ocean's vast expanse from the ship's deck, she experiences a feeling of fulfillment, knowing that she has helped someone achieve their dreams.

With a smile and a heart full of gratitude, Donella picks up the phone again, this time dialing her mentor's number. As the phone rings, she proudly shares the news of Aisha's success, knowing that it is a testament to the kindness and guidance that was passed down to her from her mentor.

Chapter Eighteen

NEW BEGINNINGS

As Donella continues her journey on the cruise ship, she unexpectedly meets someone who captures her heart in a way she never imagined. His name is Alex, and he is a charming and witty fellow crew member who shares her passion for travel and adventure.

Their initial interactions are filled with laughter and genuine connection; before long, they spend more and more time together. As they explore the ship's various destinations and share their hopes and dreams for the future, Donella begins to feel a spark of attraction growing between them.

. . .

However, as their relationship blossoms, Donella grapples with conflicting emotions. She still feels loyal to her mentor, whose guidance and support have been invaluable. She wonders how he will react to the news of her newfound romance and whether he will understand her decision to pursue happiness in her personal life.

One evening, as she sits alone on the ship's deck, Donella confides in her mentor about her feelings for Alex. With a mixture of trepidation and excitement, she dials his number and waits anxiously for him to pick up.

"Hello, sir," Donella begins, her voice filled with uncertainty. "I... I wanted to talk to you about something. I've met someone here on the ship, and... well, I think I might be falling for him."

There is a moment of silence on the other end of the line, and Donella holds her breath, waiting for her mentor's response. When he finally speaks, his voice is calm and reassuring.

. . .

"Donella, my dear," he says gently, "I'm glad to hear that you've found someone who brings you joy and happiness. But remember, love is a precious thing, and it's important to make sure that this person is truly the right one for you. Take your time and listen to your heart."

Donella feels a wave of relief wash over her as she listens to her mentor's words of wisdom. She knows that she can trust his judgment and guidance, even as she navigates the complexities of her own emotions.

With a newfound sense of clarity and confidence, Donella thanks her mentor for his support and hangs up the phone, her heart filled with gratitude for his unwavering presence in her life. As she looks ahead to the future, she knows she is ready to embrace whatever challenges and adventures lie ahead with Alex by her side.

Chapter Nineteen

TRUSTING INSTINCTS

As Donella immersed herself in her work on the cruise ship, she unexpectedly noticed the charming presence of a fellow crew member named Alex. With his easy smile and infectious enthusiasm, he brightened even the dullest days onboard.

Their paths crossed frequently as they went about their duties, exchanging friendly banter and shared glances that spoke volumes. Despite their busy schedule and the demands of their respective roles, there was an undeniable spark between them. A connection that seemed to grow stronger with each passing day.

. . .

One evening, as they found themselves alone on deck watching the sunset paint the sky in hues of pink and gold, Alex turned to Donella with a shy smile. "You know," he said softly "I've been wanting to talk to you for a while now. "

Donella's heart fluttered at his words, her cheeks flushing with a warmth she couldn't quite explain. "Really? "She replied, her voice barely above a whisper. "What about?"

Alex hesitated momentarily as if gathering his thoughts, "I've noticed how hard you work," he began, his gaze meeting hers with a newfound intensity. I just wanted to say that I admire your dedication and your passion for what You do."

A surge of emotion washed over Donella at his words, and she discovered a feeling of validation and appreciation she hadn't realized she craved. "Thank you," she said sincerely, her eyes shining with gratitude, "That means a lot coming from you."

As they stood together, bathed in the glow of the setting sun, Donella couldn't shape the feeling that this was just the beginning of something special and that with Alex by her side, anything was possible.

Chapter Twenty

LOVE AND GROWTH

Sharing moments in the days that followed, Donella found herself drawn to Alex in ways she couldn't quite explain. They shared lunches in the crew mess, stole quiet moments on deck during their breaks, and even found themselves working side by side on various tasks and projects.

With each passing day, their bond deepened, their conversations became more intimate, and their laughter more genuine. They spoke of their hopes and dreams, fears and insecurities, laying bare their hearts to one another in a terrifying and exhilarating way.

. . .

One evening, as they stood together on the deck, watching the stars twinkle overhead, Alex turned to Donella with a hesitant smile, "I have something I want to say," he began, his voice soft but determined. "I've been thinking a lot about us, about what we…"

Donella's heart skipped a beat at his words, her pulse quickening with anticipation. "What? about us?"

She asked, her voice barely above a whisper.

Alex took a deep breath, his gaze never leaving hers. "I don't want to rush things," he said earnestly, his eyes filled with a vulnerability that took her breath away, "but I can't deny the way I feel when I'm with you."

A surge of emotion washed over Donella at his words. Her heart was overflowing with the love she hadn't realized she was capable of. "I feel the same way," she confessed, her voice barely more than a whisper. "I don't know what the future holds, but I know that I want you to be a part of it."

· · ·

As they stood together, wrapped in each other's arms, Donella faced the feeling that she had finally found what she had been searching for a love that was as unexpected as it was undeniable, a love that would light her way through even the darkest of nights.

Chapter Twenty-One

JOURNEY TO CALIFORNIA

Excitement bubbled within Donella as she dialed her mentor's number, eager to share the news of her blossoming relationship with Alex. As his familiar voice greeted her on the other end of the line, she launched into an animated recount of their shared moments in heartfelt conversations.

"He's amazing," she exclaimed to De mentor, her words tumbling over each other in her eagerness to convey her feelings. "I've never met anyone like him before except you. He's kind and thoughtful, making me feel like I'm the most important person in the world."

. . .

The mentor listened intently to her words; his voice came and measured as he offered his perspective on the situation. Remember Donella, he said gently a man's love can often be measured by how he treats his mother. Take the time to visit his home, meet his family and observe his interactions with them. It will give you valuable insight into his character and values.

Donella nodded, taking his words to heart. "I understand," she replied, her voice tinged with uncertainty. "I just want to make sure I'm making the right decision."

After their conversation, Donella pondered the mentors' words as she and Alex discussed their plans for the future. When he suggested a trip to his hometown in California during their upcoming break, she saw it as the perfect opportunity to take her mentor's advice to heart.

The journey to California was filled with anticipation and excitement, the sprawling landscape unfolding before them as they made their way to Alex's hometown. As they arrived in Hollywood, Donella felt a surge of energy coursing through her veins, the pulsating heartbeat of the city echoing in her ears.

Their first stop was Alex's childhood home, where his family warmly welcomed her. Donella watched keenly as Alex interacted with his parents, siblings, and relatives, noting the love and respect that permeated their interactions.

As the days passed, Donella grew closer to Alex and his family, their bond deepening with each passing moment. As she stood before the bright lights of Hollywood, ready to embark on her audition for a movie role, she felt deeply grateful for the journey that had brought her here- and hopeful for the adventures ahead.

As she stood before the bright lights of Hollywood, Donella felt a mixture of nerves and excitement coursing through her veins. This audition was a pivotal moment in her career, a chance to prove herself on the big screen and fulfill her lifelong dream of becoming an actress.

. . .

With Alex by her side, offering words of encouragement and support, Donella stepped into the audition room with a newfound confidence. She delivered her lines with passion and conviction, pouring her heart and soul into each word as if her entire future depended on it.

As the audition came to a close, Donella couldn't shake the uncertainty lingering in the air. Had she done enough to impress the casting directors? Would this be her big break or just another missed opportunity?

Days turned into weeks as Donella anxiously awaited news of the audition. In the meantime, she immersed herself in the vibrant culture of Hollywood, exploring its iconic landmarks and soaking in the creative energy that permeated the city.

Then, one fateful afternoon, Donella received the call she had been waiting for. She had been offered the role of a lifetime, a starring role in a significant Hollywood production. A tear of joy streamed down her face as she shared the news with Alex and her mentor.

. . .

With the filming set to begin in just a few weeks, Donella threw herself into preparations with unwavering determination. She worked tirelessly to perfect and improve her craft, attending acting classes and rehearsals with a single-minded focus.

As the cameras began to roll on the set of her first feature film, Donella knew this was only the beginning of her journey to stardom.

With Alex by her side and the mentor's guidance lighting her way, she was ready to embrace whatever challenges lay ahead and make her mark on the world of Cinema.

As the sun sets on the horizon, casting a golden glow over the ocean waves, Donella stands on the deck of the cruise ship, reflecting on the incredible journey that has brought her to this moment.

From her humble beginnings in Nigeria to the bustling corridors of the cruise ship, Donella has traversed both literal and metaphorical seas, guided by her mentor's unwavering support and her family's enduring love.

She thinks back to the countless late-night conversations with her mentor, the hours spent rehearsing lines and perfecting performances, and the moments of laughter and camaraderie shared with her fellow crew members. Each experience has shaped her into the person she is today: a woman of strength, resilience, and boundless determination.

However, perhaps the most profound lesson Donella has learned along the way is the power of love and connection. From her deep bond with her mentor to her blossoming romance with Alex, Donella has discovered that love comes in many forms, each enriching her life uniquely.

As she gazes out at the vast expanse of the ocean, Donella feels gratitude wash over her. Gratitude for the opportunities she has been given, the friendships she has forged, and the love that surrounds her, both near and far.

With a smile on her face and a heart full of hope, Donella looks towards the future with excitement and anticipation. She knows that many adventures are still waiting to be had, many dreams waiting to be chased, and many lives waiting to be touched.

· · ·

As the stars twinkle overhead, illuminating the path ahead, Donella takes a deep breath and steps forward into the unknown, ready to embrace whatever new horizons await her.

Ultimately, she knows that no matter where life takes her, she will always carry with her the lessons learned, the memories made, and the love that has guided her every step of the way.

Here are a few books that share themes or elements similar to the story of Donella's journey and mentorship:

1. "The Alchemist" by Paulo Coelho - This novel follows the journey of a young shepherd named Santiago as he embarks on a quest to discover his legend and fulfill his dreams. Along the way, he encounters mentors who guide him and lessons that shape his understanding of himself and the world.

2. "Becoming" by Michelle Obama - In this memoir, former First Lady Michelle Obama reflects on her journey from her childhood in Chicago to her years

in the White House. She shares insights into the importance of mentorship, resilience, and pursuing one's passions despite obstacles.

3. "The Secret Life of Bees" by Sue Monk Kidd - Set in the 1960s American South, this novel tells the story of a young girl named Lily Owens who embarks on a journey of self-discovery and healing after escaping her troubled home life. Along the way, she finds guidance and support from unexpected mentors.

4. "The Power of One" by Bryce Courtenay - This coming-of-age novel follows the journey of a young boy named Peekay growing up in South Africa during World War II. Through his experiences and encounters with mentors, Peekay learns valuable lessons about courage, resilience, and the power of pursuing one's dreams.

5. "Educated" by Tara Westover - In this memoir, Tara Westover recounts her remarkable journey from growing up in a strict and isolated family in rural Idaho to pursuing higher education and ultimately finding her path. Along the way, she grapples with

questions of identity, self-discovery, and the importance of mentorship.

These books explore themes of personal growth, mentorship, resilience, and the pursuit of dreams, similar to the story of Donella's journey and the impact of her mentorship on others.

ACKNOWLEDGMENTS

This book was inspired by the unwavering support and encouragement of Favours Olachi Nnamdi. Your belief in me and endless encouragement have guided me throughout this journey. Thank you for inspiring me to pursue my dreams and for being a constant source of inspiration and motivation. Your friendship means the world to me.

ACKNOWLEDGMENTS

I would like to express my heartfelt gratitude to my wife and son for their unwavering support and understanding throughout the writing of this book. Your love, patience, and encouragement have been my greatest sources of strength and inspiration. Thank you for believing in me and for always being there, cheering me on every step of the way.

ACKNOWLEDGMENTS

I am deeply grateful to my mother for her endless love and unwavering support. Your boundless love has been a guiding light in my life, inspiring me to pursue my dreams and never give up. Thank you for your constant encouragement and belief in me and for always being there through thick and thin. This book is a tribute to your love and the countless sacrifices you have made for me. I am forever grateful.

ACKNOWLEDGMENTS

I extend my heartfelt appreciation to my Roommate and I @Demizicotvfilms, Journey of maidens @Demizicotvfilms, Short Comedies Facebook page: OlaEdoTv and Youtube channel: OlaEdoTv; to the Book Knock and my fellow members of the Black Authors Society for their invaluable support and encouragement. Your dedication to uplifting and celebrating black voices in literature is genuinely inspiring, and I am honored to be a part of such a vibrant community. Your feedback, discussions, and camaraderie have enriched my writing journey in ways I cannot fully express. Thank you for championing diversity, inclusion, and creativity. My gratitude to you is endless.